Best-Loved
Irish
Love Poems

First published 2025 by The O'Brien Press Ltd,
12 Terenure Road East, Rathgar, Dublin 6, D06 HD27, Ireland.
Tel: +353 1 4923333; Fax: +353 1 4922777; E-mail: books@obrien.ie; Website: obrien.ie
The O'Brien Press is a member of Publishing Ireland.

ISBN: 978-1-78849-558-5

Copyright for selection, typesetting, layout, editing, design © The O'Brien Press Ltd
Edited by Nicola Reddy.
Design and layout by Emma Byrne.

All rights reserved. No part of this publication may be reproduced or utilised in any form or by any means, electronic or mechanical, including for text and data mining, training artificial intelligence systems, photocopying, recording or in any information storage and retrieval system, without permission in writing from the publisher.

It is our understanding that the poems in this collection are in the public domain.
However, if any infringement has occurred, we ask the holder of such
copyright to contact the publisher.

1 3 5 7 8 6 4 2
25 27 29 28 26

Printed and bound by Hussar Books.

Published in
DUBLIN
UNESCO
City of Literature

Great Irish books
O'BRIEN
obrien.ie

Best-Loved Irish Love Poems

THE O'BRIEN PRESS
DUBLIN

TABLE OF CONTENTS

Far the Way That I Must Go: The poet searches for love	8
'Aedh Tells of the Perfect Beauty' by William Butler Yeats	10
'A Love Song' by Eva Gore-Booth	11
'Oh, Call It by Some Better Name' by Thomas Moore	13
'My Love, Oh, She Is My Love' translated by Douglas Hyde	14
'My Dove, My Beautiful One' by James Joyce	16
'A Mayo Love Song' by Alice Milligan	17
'The Burning-Glass' by AE (George William Russell)	18
'The Cap and Bells' by William Butler Yeats	19
'Silentium Amoris' by Oscar Wilde	21
'The Lark in the Clear Air' by Sir Samuel Ferguson	22
'The Fisherman' by Speranza (Lady Jane Wilde)	23
'Turn o'the Year' by Katharine Tynan	25
'If Thou'lt Be Mine' by Thomas Moore	26
'A White Rose' by John Boyle O'Reilly	28
'The Lone of Soul' by Dora Sigerson	29
'Aedh Wishes for the Cloths of Heaven' by William Butler Yeats	31
'Raftery's Praise of Mary Hynes' by Antoine Ó Raifteirí, translated by Lady Augusta Gregory	32
'What Is Love?' translated by Alfred Perceval Graves	35
'She' translated by Eleanor Hull	37
If I Have You, Then I Have Everything: The poet in love	38
'New Love' by Joseph Mary Plunkett	40
'This Heart That Flutters Near My Heart' by James Joyce	41
'The Heart of the Wood' translated by Lady Augusta Gregory	42
'Is It a Month' by John Millington Synge	43
'The Daisies' by James Stephens	44

'The White Birds' by William Butler Yeats	45
'Our Road' by Ethna Carbery	47
'On Stella's Birthday' by Jonathan Swift	48
'The Little Black Rose Shall Be Red at Last' by Joseph Mary Plunkett	49
'Dear Dark Head' translated by Sir Samuel Ferguson	50
'O, It Was Out by Donnycarney' by James Joyce	51
'Pulse of My Heart' translated by Charlotte Brooke	52
'Song' by Francis Ledwidge	53
'My Lagan Love' by Joseph Campbell	54
'Nocturne' by Frances Wynne	56
'Your Songs' by Joseph Mary Plunkett	58
'The Heart of the Woman' by William Butler Yeats	59
'Dark Rosaleen' by James Clarence Mangan	60
'The Cooleen' translated by Douglas Hyde	64
'Echo' by Thomas Moore	65

And Then No More: The end of love   66

'Dónal Óg (The Grief of a Girl's Heart)' translated by Lady Augusta Gregory	68
'No Second Troy' by William Butler Yeats	71
'Maire My Girl' by John Keegan Casey	72
'The Stars Stand Up in the Air' translated by Thomas MacDonagh	74
'A Song' by Francis Ledwidge	76
'Tutto è sciolto' by James Joyce	77
'In Tír-na-nÓg' by Ethna Carbery	78
'Destiny' by Speranza (Lady Jane Wilde)	80

'To ——' by Thomas Moore	83
'The Song of Wandering Aengus' by William Butler Yeats	84
'Do You Remember That Night?' translated by Eugene O'Curry	86
'Inamorata' by Francis Ledwidge	88
'When You Are Old' by William Butler Yeats	89
'The Rose of Mooncoin' by Watt Murphy	90
'The Lowlands of Flanders' by Katharine Tynan	92
''Tis the Last Rose of Summer' by Thomas Moore	94
'And Then No More' by James Clarence Mangan	96
'The Little Yellow Road' by Joseph Campbell, taken down from Mícheál Mac Ruaidhrí	98
'On Inisheer' by Ethna Carbery	100
'The Vision of Love' by AE (George William Russell)	102
'Her Voice' by Oscar Wilde	103
'My Voice' by Oscar Wilde	105
Index of first lines	106
Index of authors	108

Far the Way That I Must Go

The poet searches for love

'Aedh Tells of the Perfect Beauty'
William Butler Yeats

O cloud-pale eyelids, dream-dimmed eyes
The poets labouring all their days
To build a perfect beauty in rhyme
Are overthrown by a woman's gaze
And by the unlabouring brood of the skies:
And therefore my heart will bow, when dew
Is dropping sleep, until God burn time,
Before the unlabouring stars and you.

From The Wind Among the Reeds *(1899)*

W.B. Yeats was famously smitten with revolutionary and actress Maud Gonne; on meeting her, he declared that 'the troubling of my life began'. Around the time this poem was written, he asked Maud to marry him — not for the first time — and she said no.

'A Love Song'
Eva Gore-Booth

Like a wave that roams the sea
So lonely and so free,
Like a cloud that haunts the sky,
So distant and so high,
Like the fragrant summer wind,
So gentle and so kind,
Like a castle in the air,
So joyous and so fair,
Like a lily by the wall,
So golden and so tall,
Gay as any flower that blows,
Splendid as a sun-lit rose,
Bright and bravely blossoming,
Is my Lady of the Spring.
Fair of face, and clear of sight,
Living always in the light,
Valorous and free and strong
As the wind's courageous song,
All of magic sunshine made,
Secret as a forest glade,
Silver-lit beneath dark trees
By pale-starred anemones,
Fair as that white dawn that gleams
Through the ivory gate of dreams,
Glorious to gaze upon,

With strange lights of summers gone,
Silver of bright daisies stored,
Smallest change in summer's hoard,
Gold of vanished daffodils,
Is my Lady of the Hills.
The grace of all things gay,
The joy of a swallow's flight,
The light of a summer's day,
The peace of a moon-lit night,
All the strength, and the hope, and the gladness of living are hers,
And her voice is the voice of the wind in a forest of firs.

From Poems *(1898)*

As well as being a writer, Eva Gore-Booth was a political activist who fought tirelessly for women's rights, as did her sister, Constance (Countess Markievicz).

'Oh, Call It by Some Better Name'
Thomas Moore

Oh, call it by some better name,
   For Friendship sounds too cold,
While Love is now a worldly flame,
   Whose shrine must be of gold;
And Passion, like the sun at noon,
   That burns o'er all he sees,
Awhile as warm, will set as soon –
   Then, call it none of these.

Imagine something purer far,
   More free from stain of clay
Than Friendship, Love, or Passion are,
   Yet human still as they:
And if thy lip, for love like this,
   No mortal word can frame,
Go, ask of angels what it is,
   And call it by that name.

From The Poetical Works of Thomas Moore (1840–1841)

Born in Dublin, Tom Moore was a musician and lyricist whose collection Irish Melodies *was incredibly famous in the early 1800s.*

'My Love, Oh, She Is My Love'
Anon, translated from the Irish by Douglas Hyde

She casts a spell, oh, casts a spell!
Which haunts me more than I can tell.
Dearer, because she makes me ill
Than who would will to make me well.

She is my store! oh, she my store!
Whose grey eye wounded me so sore,
Who will not place in mine her palm,
Nor love, nor calm me any more.

She is my pet, oh, she my pet!
Whom I can never more forget;
Who would not lose by me one moan,
Nor stone upon my cairn would set.

She is my roon, oh, she my roon!
Who tells me nothing, leaves me soon;
Who would not lose by me one sigh,
Were death and I within one room.

She is my dear, oh, she my dear!
Who cares not whether I be here.
Who will not weep when I am dead,
But makes me shed the silent tear.

Hard my case, oh, hard my case!
For in her eye no hope I trace,
She will not hear me any more,
But I adore her silent face.

She is my choice, oh, she my choice!
Who never made me to rejoice;
Who caused my heart to ache so oft,
Who put no softness in her voice.

Great my grief, oh, great my grief!
Neglected, scorned beyond belief,
By her who looks at me askance,
By her who grants me no relief.

She's my desire, oh, my desire!
More glorious than the bright sun's fire;
Who were than wild-blown ice more cold
Were I so bold as to sit by her.

She it is who stole my heart,
And left a void and aching smart;
But if she soften not her eye,
I know that life and I must part.

From Anthology of Irish Verse, *ed. Padraic Colum (1922)*

Douglas Hyde, known also as An Craoibhín Aoibhinn *('the Sweet Little Branch') was an academic and politician who served as the first president of Ireland from 1938 to 1945.*

'My Dove, My Beautiful One'
James Joyce

My dove, my beautiful one,
  Arise, arise!
  The night-dew lies
Upon my lips and eyes.

The odorous winds are weaving
  A music of sighs:
  Arise, arise,
My dove, my beautiful one!

I wait by the cedar tree,
  My sister, my love.
  White breast of the dove,
My breast shall be your bed.

The pale dew lies
  Like a veil on my head.
  My fair one, my fair dove,
Arise, arise!

From Chamber Music *(1907)*

This collection of thirty-six poems was Joyce's first published book. He later commented in a letter to his wife, Nora Barnacle, 'When I wrote it, I was a lonely boy, walking about by myself at night and thinking that one day a girl would love me.'

'A Mayo Love Song'
Alice Milligan

It is far, and it is far,
To Connemara where you are,
To where its purple glens enfold you
As glooming heavens that hold a star.

But they shall shine, they yet shall shine,
Colleen, those eyes of yours on mine
Like stars that after eve assemble,
And tremble over the mountain line.

Though it be far, though it be far,
I'll journey over to where you are,
By grasslands green that lie between
And shining lakes at Mullingar.

And we shall be, and we shall be,
Oh, colleen lonely, beloved by me,
For evermore on a moor of Mayo
'Mid heather singing like the sea.

From Hero Lays *(1908)*

Alice Milligan was a lifelong campaigner for the Irish language and the cause of Irish freedom. With fellow writer Ethna Carbery, she edited influential nationalist magazine The Shan Van Vocht.

'The Burning-Glass'
AE (George William Russell)

A shaft of fire that falls like dew,
   And melts and maddens all my blood,
From out thy spirit flashes through
   The burning-glass of womanhood.

Only so far; here must I stay:
   Nearer I miss the light, the fire;
I must endure the torturing ray,
   And with all beauty, all desire.

Ah, time long must the effort be,
   And far the way that I must go
To bring my spirit unto thee,
   Behind the glass, within the glow.

From Collected Poems by AE *(1913)*

George William 'AE' Russell was a hugely influential painter, philosopher and organiser. He was also a mystic who claimed to have experienced visions of past lives and other worlds, which he attempted to capture in his art.

'The Cap and Bells'
William Butler Yeats

The jester walked in the garden:
The garden had fallen still;
He bade his soul rise upward
And stand on her window-sill.

It rose in a straight blue garment,
When owls began to call:
It had grown wise-tongued by thinking
Of a quiet and light footfall;

But the young queen would not listen;
She rose in her pale night gown;
She drew in the heavy casement
And pushed the latches down.

He bade his heart go to her,
When the owls called out no more;
In a red and quivering garment
It sang to her through the door.

It had grown sweet-tongued by dreaming,
Of a flutter of flower-like hair;
But she took up her fan from the table
And waved it off on the air.

'I have cap and bells,' he pondered,
'I will send them to her and die;'
And when the morning whitened
He left them where she went by.

She laid them upon her bosom,
Under a cloud of her hair,
And her red lips sang them a love-song:
Till stars grew out of the air.

She opened her door and her window,
And the heart and the soul came through,
To her right hand came the red one,
To her left hand came the blue.

They set up a noise like crickets,
A chattering wise and sweet,
And her hair was a folded flower
And the quiet of love in her feet.

First published in The National Observer *(1894)*

Yeats claimed not to understand the meaning of this poem because it was written for him by ghosts. He said that he 'dreamed this story exactly as I have written it'.

'Silentium Amoris'
Oscar Wilde

As oftentimes the too resplendent sun
   Hurries the pallid and reluctant moon
Back to her sombre cave, 'ere she hath won
   A single ballad from the nightingale,
   So doth thy Beauty make my lips to fail,
And all my sweetest singing out of tune.

And as at dawn across the level mead
   On wings impetuous some wind will come,
And with its too harsh kisses break the reed
   Which was its only instrument of song,
   So my too stormy passions work me wrong,
And for excess of Love my Love is dumb.

But surely unto Thee mine eyes did show
   Why I am silent, and my lute unstrung;
Else it were better we should part, and go,
   Thou to some lips of sweeter melody,
   And I to nurse the barren memory
Of unkissed kisses, and songs never sung.

From Poems *(1881)*

The title of this poem translates to 'The Silence of Love'. In his own poem 'Two Loves', Wilde's lover Lord Alfred Douglas referred to 'the love that dare not speak its name' — words that would be brought up at Wilde's trial for homosexual acts.

'The Lark in the Clear Air'
Sir Samuel Ferguson

Dear thoughts are in my mind
And my soul soars enchanted,
As I hear the sweet lark sing
In the clear air of the day.
For a tender beaming smile
To my hope has been granted,
And tomorrow she shall hear
All my fond heart would say.

I shall tell her all my love,
All my soul's adoration;
And I think she will hear me,
And will not say me nay.
It is this that gives my soul
All its joyous elation,
As I hear the sweet lark sing
In the clear air of the day.

From The Irish Song Book, *ed. Alfred Perceval Graves (1895)*

Samuel Ferguson wrote these lyrics to accompany an elusive, ancient Irish air which had been sung to his wife, Lady Mary, many years before.

'The Fisherman'

Speranza (Lady Jane Wilde)

I.

The water rushes — the water foams —
A fisherman sat on the bank,
And calmly gazed on his flowing line,
As it down in the deep wave sank,
The water rushes — the water foams —
The bright waves part asunder,
And with wondering eyes he sees arise
A nymph from the caverns under.

II.

She sprang to him — she sang to him —
Ah! wherefore dost thou tempt
With thy deadly food, my bright-scaled brood
From out their crystal element?
Could'st thou but know our joy below,
Thou would'st leave the harsh, cold land,
And dwell in our caves 'neath the glittering waves,
As lord of our sparkling band.

III.

See you not now the bright sun bow
To gaze on his form here;
And the pale moon's face wears a softer grace
In the depths of our silver sphere.

See the fleecy shroud of the azure cloud
In the heaven beneath the sea;
And look at thine eyes, what a glory lies
In their lustre. Come, look with me.

IV.

The water rushes – the water foams –
The cool wave kiss'd his feet.
The maiden's eyes were like azure skies,
And her voice was low and sweet.
She sung to him – she clung to him –
O'er the glittering stream they lean;
Half drew she him, half sunk he in,
And never more was seen.

From Poems by Speranza *(1871)*

Lady Jane Wilde was a folklorist and campaigner whose literary salons at No 1 Merrion Square were the heart of cultural life in 19th century Dublin.

'Turn o' the Year'
Katharine Tynan

This is the time when bit by bit
The days begin to lengthen sweet,
And every minute gained is joy —
And love stirs in the heart of a boy.

This is the time the sun, of late
Content to lie abed till eight,
Lifts up betimes his sleepy head —
And love stirs in the heart of a maid.

This is the time we dock the night
Of a whole hour of candlelight;
When song of linnet and thrush is heard —
And love stirs in the heart of a bird.

This is the time when sword-blades green,
With gold and purple damascene,
Pierce the brown crocus-bed a-row —
And love stirs in a heart I know.

From The Wind in the Trees *(1898)*

Over fifty years, Katharine Tynan wrote more than a dozen collections of poetry, five autobiographies and a hundred novels. Her poetry often looked at domesticity, motherhood and country life.

'If Thou'lt Be Mine'
Thomas Moore

If thou'lt be mine, the treasures of air,
Of earth, and sea, shall lie at thy feet;
Whatever in Fancy's eye looks fair,
Or in Hope's sweet music sounds most sweet,
Shall be ours — if thou wilt be mine, love!

Bright flowers shall bloom wherever we rove,
A voice divine shall talk in each stream;
The stars shall look like worlds of love,
And this earth be all one beautiful dream
In our eyes — if thou wilt be mine, love!

And thoughts, whose source is hidden and high,
Like streams that come from heaven-ward hills,
Shall keep our hearts, like meads, that lie
To be bathed by those eternal rills,
Ever green, if thou wilt be mine, love!

All this and more the Spirit of Love
Can breathe o'er them who feel his spells;
That heaven, which forms his home above,
He can make on earth, wherever he dwells,
As thou'lt own — if thou wilt be mine, love!

From The Irish Melodies *(1808–1834)*

Thomas Moore began composing lyrics to be sung to the tunes of old Irish folk songs in 1808. **Irish Melodies** *eventually ran to ten volumes and earned him the lifelong nickname of 'Melody Moore'.*

'A White Rose'
John Boyle O'Reilly

The red rose whispers of passion,
   And the white rose breathes of love;
O, the red rose is a falcon,
   And the white rose is a dove.

But I send you a cream-white rosebud
   With a flush on its petal tips;
For the love that is purest and sweetest
   Has a kiss of desire on the lips.

From In Bohemia *(1886)*

John Boyle O'Reilly was sentenced to twenty years in prison for membership of the IRB. He escaped from a penal colony in Australia and made his way to America, where he became a successful journalist and editor.

'The Lone of Soul'
Dora Sigerson

The world has many lovers, but the one
   She loves the best is he within whose heart
She but half-reigning queen and mistress is;
   Whose lonely soul for ever stands apart,

Who from her face will ever turn away,
   Who but half-hearing listens to her voice,
Whose heart beats to her passion, but whose soul
   Within her presence never will rejoice.

What land has let the dreamer from its gates,
   What face beloved hides from him away?
A dreamer outcast from some world of dreams –
   He goes for ever lonely on his way.

The wedded body and the single soul,
   Beside his mate he shall most mateless stand,
For ever to dream of that unseen face –
   For ever to sigh for that enchanted land.

Like a great pine upon some Alpine height,
   Torn by the winds and bent beneath the snow,
Half overthrown by icy avalanche,
   The lone of soul throughout the world must go.

Alone among his kind he stands alone,
  Torn by the passions of his own strange heart,
Stoned by continual wreckage of his dreams,
  He in the crowd for ever is apart.

Like the great pine that, rocking no sweet nest,
  Swings no young birds to sleep upon the bough,
But where the raven only comes to croak —
  'There lives no man more desolate than thou!'

So goes the lone of soul amid the world —
  No love upon his breast, with singing, cheers;
But sorrow builds her home within his heart,
  And, nesting there, will rear her brood of tears.

From Ballads and Poems *(1899)*

As well as being a talented and prolific writer, Dora Sigerson was a gifted sculptor. Her most famous work is the 1916 memorial just inside the front gates of Glasnevin Cemetery, where she is also buried.

'Aedh Wishes for the Cloths of Heaven'
William Butler Yeats

Had I the heavens' embroidered cloths,
Enwrought with golden and silver light,
The blue and the dim and the dark cloths
Of night and light and the half-light,
I would spread the cloths under your feet:
But I, being poor, have only my dreams;
I have spread my dreams under your feet;
Tread softly because you tread on my dreams.

From The Wind Among the Reeds *(1899)*

According to his biographer Joseph Hone, Yeats once commented that his poem 'The Cap and Bells' (p19) is 'the way to win a lady' while this poem is 'the way to lose one'.

'Raftery's Praise of Mary Hynes'
Antoine Ó Raifteirí, translated by Lady Augusta Gregory

Going to Mass by the will of God,
The day came wet and the wind rose;
I met Mary Hynes at the cross of Kiltartan,
And I fell in love with her there and then.

I spoke to her kind and mannerly,
As by report was her own way;
And she said, 'Raftery, my mind is easy,
You may come to-day to Baile-laoi.'

When I heard her offer I did not linger;
When her talk went to my heart my heart rose.
We had only to go across the three fields,
We had daylight with us to Baile-laoi.

The table was laid with glasses and a quart measure;
She had fair hair and she sitting beside me;
And she said, 'Drink, Raftery, and a hundred welcomes;
There is a strong cellar in Baile-laoi.'

O star of light and O sun in harvest;
O amber hair, O my share of the world!
Will you come with me on the Sunday,
Till we agree together before all the people?

I would not begrudge you a song every Sunday evening;
Punch on the table or wine if you would drink it.
But, O King of Glory, dry the roads before me
Till I find the way to Baile-laoi.

There is sweet air on the side of the hill,
When you are looking down upon Baile-laoi;
When you are walking in the valley picking nuts and
　　blackberries,
There is music of the birds in it and music of the Sidhe.

What is the worth of greatness till you have the light
Of the flower of the branch that is by your side?
There is no good to deny it or to try and hide it;
She is the sun in the heavens who wounded my heart.

There was no part in Ireland I did not travel,
From the rivers to the tops of the mountains;
To the edge of Loch Greine whose mouth is hidden,
And I saw no beauty but was behind hers.

Her hair was shining and her brows were shining too;
Her face was like herself, her mouth pleasant and sweet;
She is the pride and I give her the branch,
She is the shining flower of Baile-laoi.

It is Mary Hynes, the calm and easy woman,
Has beauty in her mind and in her face.
If a hundred clerks were gathered together,
They could not write down a half of her ways.

From The Kiltartan Poetry Book *(1918)*

Antoine Ó Raifteirí was known as the last of the wandering bards. Blind since childhood, he performed songs and recited poems at the houses of the landed gentry.

'What Is Love?'
Anon, translated from the Early Irish by Alfred Perceval Graves

A love all-commanding, all-withstanding
   Through a year is my love;
A grief darkly hiding, starkly biding
   Without let or remove;
Of strength a sharp straining, past sustaining
   Wheresoever I rove,
A force still extending without ending
   Before and around and above.

Of Heaven 'tis the brightest amazement,
   The blackest abasement of Hell,
A struggle for breath with a spectre,
   In nectar a choking to death;
'Tis a race with Heaven's lightning and thunder,
   Then champion feats under Moyle's water:
'Tis pursuing the cuckoo, the wooing
   Of echo, the Rock's airy daughter.

Till my red lips turn ashen,
   My light limbs grow leaden,
My heart loses motion,
   In Death my eyes deaden,
So is my love and my passion,
So is my ceaseless devotion

To her to whom I gave them,
To her who will not have them.

From The Book of Irish Poetry *(1915)*

A passionate folklorist, Alfred Perceval Graves always tried to 'treat Irish in an Irish way', keeping the unusual structure and metre of the Irish language in his translations.

'She'

Anon, translated from the Irish by Eleanor Hull

The white bloom of the blackthorn, she,
  The small sweet raspberry-blossom, she;
More fair the shy, rare glance of her eye,
  Than the wealth of the world to me.

My heart's pulse, my secret, she,
  The flower of the fragrant apple, she;
A summer glow o'er the winter's snow,
  'Twixt Christmas and Easter, she.

From The Poem Book of the Gael *(1912)*

In Irish mythology, the blackthorn tree was associated with the leanán sídhe, a beautiful fairy who inspires musicians and artists, at the price of their lives.

If I Have You, Then I Have Everything

The poet in love

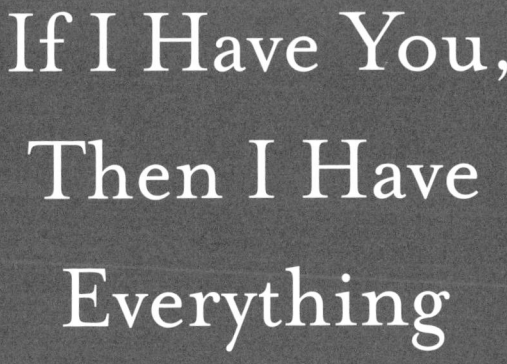

'New Love'
Joseph Mary Plunkett

The day I knew you loved me we had lain
Deep in Coill Doraca down by Gleann na Scath
Unknown to each till suddenly I saw
You in the shadow, knew oppressive pain
Stopping my heart, and there you did remain
In dreadful beauty fair without a flaw,
Blinding the eyes that yet could not withdraw
Till wild between us drove the wind and rain.

Breathless we reached the brugh before the west
Burst in full fury – then with lightning stroke
The tempest in my heart roared up and broke
Its barriers, and I swore I would not rest
Till that mad heart was worthy of your breast
Or dead for you – and then this love awoke.

From The Poems of Joseph Mary Plunkett *(1916)*

Joseph Mary Plunkett was one of the leaders of the 1916 Rising and a signatory of the Proclamation. He married his love, artist Grace Gifford, in Kilmainham Gaol just a few hours before his execution.

'This Heart That Flutters Near My Heart'
James Joyce

This heart that flutters near my heart
  My hope and all my riches is,
Unhappy when we draw apart
  And happy between kiss and kiss;
My hope and all my riches – yes! –
And all my happiness.

For there, as in some mossy nest
  The wrens will divers treasures keep,
I laid those treasures I possessed
  Ere that mine eyes had learned to weep.
Shall we not be as wise as they
Though love live but a day?

From Chamber Music *(1907)*

James Joyce felt that the poems in this collection were 'pretty enough to be put to music'. Over the years, artists including Syd Barrett, Mercury Rev, Julian Lennon, Gavin Friday and Judith Hill have released their own musical interpretations.

'The Heart of the Wood'
Anon, translated from the Irish by Lady Augusta Gregory

My hope and my love,
we will go for a while into the wood,
scattering the dew,
where we will see the trout,
we will see the blackbird on its nest;
the deer and the buck calling,
the little bird that is sweetest
singing on the branches;
the cuckoo on the top of the fresh green;
and death will never come near us
for ever in the sweet wood.

From The Kiltartan Poetry Book *(1918)*

Lady Gregory learned Irish as an adult from her tenants and the locals of Kiltartan, County Galway, and went on to collect and translate poems and stories that may otherwise have been lost to time.

'Is It a Month'
John Millington Synge

Is it a month since I and you
In the starlight of Glen Dubh
Stretched beneath a hazel bough
Kissed from ear and throat to brow,
Since your fingers, neck, and chin
Made the bars that fenced me in,
Till Paradise seemed but a wreck
Near your bosom, brow, and neck,
And stars grew wilder, growing wise,
In the splendour of your eyes!
Since the weasel wandered near
Whilst we kissed from ear to ear
And the wet and withered leaves
Blew about your cap and sleeves,
Till the moon sank tired through the ledge
Of the wet and windy hedge?
And we took the starry lane
Back to Dublin town again.

From J.M. Synge Collected Works, Volume I: Poems (1962)

Synge is best known as the playwright behind The Playboy of the Western World, *now considered a modern classic but which in 1907 caused riots on its opening night due to its perceived immorality.*

'The Daisies'

James Stephens

In the scented bud of the morning – O,
  When the windy grass went rippling far,
I saw my dear one walking slow,
  In the field where the daisies are.

We did not laugh and we did not speak
  As we wandered happily to and fro;
I kissed my dear on either cheek,
  In the bud of the morning – O.

A lark sang up from the breezy land,
  A lark sang down from a cloud afar,
And she and I went hand in hand
  In the field where the daisies are.

From Songs from the Clay *(1915)*

James Joyce was an admirer of this poet and novelist and once suggested that Stephens might help him to finish Finnegans Wake. *He said the book could be credited to JJ & S, for the Jameses Joyce & Stephens (and a play on the whiskey brand John Jameson & Sons).*

'The White Birds'
William Butler Yeats

I would that we were, my beloved, white birds on the foam
 of the sea!
We tire of the flame of the meteor, before it can fade and
 flee;
And the flame of the blue star of twilight, hung low on the
 rim of the sky,
Has awakened in our hearts, my beloved, a sadness that
 may not die.

A weariness comes from those dreamers, dew-dabbled, the
 lily and rose;
Ah, dream not of them, my beloved, the flame of the
 meteor that goes,
Or the flame of the blue star that lingers hung low in the
 fall of the dew:
For I would we were changed to white birds on the
 wandering foam: I and you!

I am haunted by numberless islands, and many a Danaan
 shore,
Where Time would surely forget us, and Sorrow come near
 us no more;
Soon far from the rose and the lily and fret of the flames
 would we be,

Were we only white birds, my beloved, buoyed out on the foam of the sea!

From The Rose *(1893)*

W.B. Yeats wrote this poem for his muse Maud Gonne, who told him during a walk by the cliffs of Howth, County Dublin, that seagulls were her favourite birds.

'Our Road'
Ethna Carbery

Here is the road that you must climb with me,
This road that winds between the hill and sea,
And leads to where our quiet home shall be.

Love waits us there – not proud, nor kingly clad,
Oh! just a little joyous country lad,
With tender wiles to make our tired hearts glad.

No barbéd arrow doth he hold for us –
But outstretched hands, divine and generous.
Would all sad wayfarers were welcomed thus!

The world hath tortured – yet immense our gain
To find enduring peace around us twain,
I, weary of my wanderings, you of your disdain.

From The Four Winds of Eirinn *(1902)*

This poetry collection by Ethna Carbery, whose real name was Anna Johnston, was edited and published posthumously by her husband, poet Seumas MacManus. It was incredibly popular and reprinted ten times in its first year alone, making her the most widely read poet in Ireland at the time.

'On Stella's Birthday'
Jonathan Swift

Stella this day is thirty four,
(We won't dispute a year or more)
However Stella, be not troubled,
Although thy size and years are doubled,
Since first I saw thee at sixteen
The brightest virgin of the Green,
So little is thy form declin'd
Made up so largely in thy mind.
Oh, would it please the gods to split
Thy beauty, size, and years, and wit,
No age could furnish out a pair
Of nymphs so graceful, wise and fair
With half the lustre of your eyes,
With half thy wit, thy years and size:
And then before it grew too late,
How should I beg of gentle Fate,
(That either nymph might have her swain,)
To split my worship too in twain.

First published in 1719

'Stella' was Jonathan Swift's name for his muse, Esther Johnson. The nature of their relationship — were they married, friends, secretly related? — is a mystery for the ages.

'The Little Black Rose Shall Be Red at Last'
Joseph Mary Plunkett

Because we share our sorrows and our joys
And all your dear and intimate thoughts are mine
We shall not fear the trumpets and the noise
Of battle, for we know our dreams divine,
And when my heart is pillowed on your heart
And ebb and flowing of their passionate flood
Shall beat in concord love through every part
Of brain and body – when at last the blood
O'er leaps the final barrier to find
Only one source wherein to spend its strength
And we two lovers, long but one in mind
And soul, are made one only flesh at length;
Praise God if this my blood fulfils the doom
When you, dark rose, shall redden into bloom.

From The Poems of Joseph Mary Plunkett *(1916)*

This poem is dedicated to Caitlín ní hUllacháin, the personification of Ireland and a symbol of the Irish nationalist movement.

'Dear Dark Head'

Anon, translated from the Irish by Sir Samuel Ferguson

Put your head, darling, darling, darling,
Your darling black head my heart above;
Oh, mouth of honey, with the thyme for fragrance,
Who with heart in breast could deny you love?

Oh, many and many a young girl for me is pining,
Letting her locks of gold to the cold wind free,
For me, the foremost of our gay young fellows;
But I'd leave a hundred, pure love, for thee!

Then put your head, darling, darling, darling,
Your darling black head my heart above;
Oh, mouth of honey, with the thyme for fragrance,
Who, with heart in breast, could deny you love?

First published in 1867

This is Samuel Ferguson's thoughtful translation of an 18th century love song, 'Ceann Dubh Dilis' which, according to Padraic Colum, 'carries into English the Gaelic music and the Gaelic feeling'.

'O, It Was Out by Donnycarney'

James Joyce

O, it was out by Donnycarney
   When the bat flew from tree to tree
My love and I did walk together;
   And sweet were the words she said to me.

Along with us the summer wind
   Went murmuring – O, happily! –
But softer than the breath of summer
   Was the kiss she gave to me.

From Chamber Music *(1907)*

In contrast to James Joyce's most famous novel, Ulysses, *there is only one overt mention of Ireland in this poetry collection. Donnycarney is a northside Dublin suburb not far from where the Joyce family lived at the turn of the 20th century.*

'Pulse of My Heart'

Anon, translated from the Irish by Charlotte Brooke

As the sweet blackberry's modest bloom,
Fair flowering, greets the sight;
Or strawberries, in their rich perfume,
Fragrance and bloom unite:
So this fair plant of tender youth,
In outward charms can vie,
And, from within, the soul of truth
Soft beaming, fills her eye.

Pulse of my heart! – dear source of care,
Stolen sighs, and love-breathed vows!
Sweeter than when, through scented air,
Gay bloom the apple boughs!
With thee no days can winter seem,
Nor frost, nor blast can chill;
Thou the soft breeze, the cheering beam
That keeps it summer still!

From Reliques of Irish Poetry *(1789)*

The publication of Charlotte Brooks's collection marked a turning point in Irish literature. It was the first time a significant number of Irish poems were presented for an English-speaking audience and is seen as the precursor to the Irish Literary Revival.

'Song'
Francis Ledwidge

Nothing but sweet music wakes
   My Beloved, my Beloved.
Sleeping by the blue lakes,
   My own Beloved!

Song of lark and song of thrush,
   My Beloved! my Beloved!
Sing in morning's rosy bush,
   My own Beloved!

When your eyes dawn blue and clear,
   My Beloved! my Beloved!
You will find me waiting here,
   My own Beloved!

From Songs of Peace *(1917)*

This collection of poems was fully drafted when Francis Ledwidge died at the third battle of Ypres. It was published posthumously by his friend and benefactor Lord Dunsany.

'My Lagan Love'
Joseph Campbell

Where Lagan stream sings lullaby
There blows a lily fair:
The twilight-gleam is in her eye,
The night is on her hair.
And, like a love-sick *leanan-sidhe*,
She hath my heart in thrall:
Nor life I owe, nor liberty,
For Love is lord of all.

Her father sails a running-barge
'Twixt Leamh-beag and The Druim;
And on the lonely river-marge
She elears his hearth for him.
When she was only fairy-high
Her gentle mother died;
But dew-Love keeps her memory
Green on the Lagan-side.

And oft-times when the beetle's horn
Hath lulled the eve to sleep,
I steal unto her shieling lorn,
And thro' the dooring peep.
There on the crickets' singing stone
She spares the bogwood fire,

And hums in sad, sweet under-tone
The song of heart's desire.

Her welcome, like her love for me,
Is from her heart within:
Her warm kiss is felicity,
That knows no taint of sin.
And when I stir my foot to go,
'Tis leaving Love and light
To feel the wind of longing blow
From out the dark of night.

Where Lagan stream sings lullaby
There blooms a lily fair:
The twilight-gleam is in her eye,
The night is on her hair.
And like a love-sick *leanan-sidhe*,
She hath my heart in thrall:
Nor life I owe, nor liberty,
For Love is lord of all.

From Songs of Uladh *(1904)*

This poem was written to a traditional air that had been collected in Donegal by Campbell's collaborator Herbert Hughes. As a song, it has been covered by countless artists, beginning with tenor John McCormack in 1910.

'Nocturne'
Frances Wynne

    The long day was bright,
It slowly passed from the purple slopes of the hill;
    And then the night
Came floating quietly down, and the world grew still.

    Now I lie awake,
The south wind stirs the white curtains to and fro.
    Cries the corncrake
In fields that stretch by the stream-side, misty and low.

    At the meadow's edge
I know the faint pink clover is heavy with dew.
    Under the hedge
The speedwell closes its sweet eyes, dreamily blue.

    With pursed rosy lips
The baby buds are asleep on the apple tree.
    The river slips
Beneath the scarcely swayed willows, on to the sea.

    The dark grows, and grows,
But I'm too happy to sleep, and the reason why
    No creature knows,
Save certain little brown birds, and my love, and I.

From Whisper! *(1891)*

County Louth poet Frances Wynne died just two years after the publication of her only poetry collection. Her friend and fellow author Katharine Tynan said she 'drunk deep of the cup of life she had seized so eagerly, as if she knew there was not much time'.

'Your Songs'
Joseph Mary Plunkett

If I have you then I have everything
In One, and that One nothing of them all
Nor all compounded, and within the wall
Beneath the tower I wait to hear you sing:
Love breathing low above the breast of Spring,
Pressing her heart with baby heart and small
From baby lips love-syllables lets fall
And strokes with gentle hand her quivering wing.

You come rejoicing all the wilderness,
Filling with praise the land to joy unknown,
Fresh from that garden whose perfumes have blown
Down through the valley of the cypresses —
O heart, you know not your own loveliness,
Nor these your songs, for they are yours alone.

From The Poems of Joseph Mary Plunkett *(1916)*

Not only a devotee of the Irish language, Plunkett was also passionate about the 'supra-national' language Esperanto and even co-founded the Irish Esperanto League.

'The Heart of the Woman'
William Butler Yeats

O what to me the little room
That was brimmed up with prayer and rest;
He bade me out into the gloom,
And my breast lies upon his breast.

O what to me my mother's care,
The house where I was safe and warm;
The shadowy blossom of my hair
Will hide us from the bitter storm.

O hiding hair and dewy eyes,
I am no more with life and death,
My heart upon his warm heart lies,
My breath is mixed into his breath.

From The Wind Among the Reeds *(1899)*

This seemingly simple poem is peppered with hints about the darkness and danger of love and devotion. The year before it was written, W.B. Yeats and Maud Gonne had entered into a 'spiritual marriage' — but she continued to refuse a real one.

'Dark Rosaleen'

James Clarence Mangan

O my Dark Rosaleen,
Do no sigh, do not weep!
The priests are on the ocean green,
They march along the deep.
There's wine from the royal Pope,
Upon the ocean green;
And Spanish ale shall give you hope,
My Dark Rosaleen!
My own Rosaleen!
Shall glad your heart, shall give you hope,
Shall give you health, and help, and hope,
My Dark Rosaleen.

Over hills, and thro' dales,
Have I roamed for your sake;
All yesterday I sailed with sails
On river and on lake.
The Erne at its highest flood,
I dashed across unseen,
For there was lightning in my blood,
My Dark Rosaleen!
My own Rosaleen!
O there was lightning in my blood,
Red lightning lightened thro' my blood,
My Dark Rosaleen!

All day long, in unrest,
To and fro, do I move.
The very soul within my breast
Is wasted for you, love!
The heart in my bosom faints
To think of you, my queen,
My life of life, my saint of saints,
My Dark Rosaleen!
My own Rosaleen!
To hear your sweet and sad complaints,
My life, my love, my saint of saints,
My Dark Rosaleen!

Woe and pain, pain and woe,
Are my lot, night and noon,
To see your bright face clouded so,
Like to the mournful moon.
But yet will I rear your throne
Again in golden sheen;
'Tis you shall reign, shall reign alone,
My Dark Rosaleen!
My own Rosaleen!
'Tis you shall have the golden throne,
'Tis you shall reign, shall reign alone,
My Dark Rosaleen!

Over dews, over sands,
Will I fly for your weal:
Your holy delicate white hands
Shall girdle me with steel.
At home in your emerald bowers,
From morning's dawn till e'en,
You'll pray for me, my flower of flowers,
My Dark Rosaleen!
My fond Rosaleen!
You'll think of me thro' daylight hours,
My virgin flower, my flower of flowers,
My Dark Rosaleen!

I could scale the blue air,
I could plough the high hills,
O I could kneel all night in prayer,
To heal your many ills!
And one beamy smile from you
Would float like light between
My toils and me, my own, my true,
My Dark Rosaleen!
My fond Rosaleen!
Would give me life and soul anew,
A second life, a soul anew,
My Dark Rosaleen!

O the Erne shall run red
With redundance of blood,
The earth shall rock beneath our tread,
And flames wrap hill and wood,
And gun-peal and slogan cry
Wake many a glen serene,
Ere you shall fade, ere you shall die,
My Dark Rosaleen!
My own Rosaleen!
The Judgement Hour must first be nigh,
Ere you can fade, ere you can die,
My Dark Rosaleen!

From James Clarence Mangan: His Selected Poems *(1897)*

This love poem to Ireland is based on an old balled called 'Róisín Dubh'. Mangan wrote two other translations, 'Little Black-Haired Rose' and 'Black-Haired Fair Rose', before landing on this classic interpretation.

'The Cooleen'

Anonymous, translated from the Irish by Douglas Hyde

A honey mist on a day of frost, in a dark oak wood,
And love for thee in the heart of me, thou bright, white, and good,
Thy slender form, soft and warm, thy red lips apart,
Thou hast found me, and hast bound me, and put grief in my heart.

In fair-green and market, men mark thee, bright, young and merry,
Though thou hurt them like foes with the rose of thy blush of the berry;
Her cheeks are a poppy, her eye it is Cupid's helper,
But each foolish man dreams that its beams for himself are.

Whoe'er saw the Cooleen in a cool dewy meadow
On a morning in summer in sunshine and shadow:
All the young men go wild for her, my childeen, my treasure,
But now let them mope, they've no hope to possess her.

Let us roam, O my darling, afar through the mountains,
Drink milk of the goat, wine and bulcán in fountains;
With music and play every day from my lyre,
And leave to come rest on my breast when you tire.

From Love Songs of Connaught *(1909)*

This love poem to a fair-haired girl (chúilfhionn) has been in existence in various forms for centuries. It is often accompanied by a beautiful and ancient Irish air.

'Echo'
Thomas Moore

How sweet the answer Echo makes
  To Music at night,
When, roused by lute or horn, she wakes,
And far away, o'er lawns and lakes,
  Goes answering light.

Yet Love hath echoes truer far,
  And far more sweet,
Than e'er beneath the moonlight's star,
Of horn, or lute, or soft guitar,
  The songs repeat.

'Tis when the sigh, in youth sincere,
  And only then —
The sigh that's breathed for one to hear,
Is by that one, that only dear,
  Breathed back again!

From The Irish Melodies *(1808–1834)*

Known for the success of this poetry collection, in the 1820s Moore was — unfairly, it seems — implicated in the destruction of Lord Byron's unpublished memoirs, now seen as one of the greatest crimes in literary history.

And Then No More

The end of love

'Dónal Óg (The Grief of a Girl's Heart)'
Anon, translated from the Irish by Lady Augusta Gregory

O Dónal óg, if you go across the sea,
bring myself with you and do not forget it;
and you will have a sweetheart for fair days and market days,
and the daughter of the King of Greece beside you at night.

It is late last night the dog was speaking of you;
the snipe was speaking of you in her deep marsh.
It is you are the lonely bird through the woods;
and that you may be without a mate until you find me.

You promised me, and you said a lie to me,
that you would be before me where the sheep are flocked;
I gave a whistle and three hundred cries to you,
and I found nothing there but a bleating lamb.

You promised me a thing that was hard for you,
a ship of gold under a silver mast;
twelve towns with a market in all of them,
and a fine white court by the side of the sea.

You promised me a thing that is not possible,
that you would give me gloves of the skin of a fish;
that you would give me shoes of the skin of a bird;
and a suit of the dearest silk in Ireland.

O Dónal óg, it is I would be better to you
than a high, proud, spendthrift lady:
I would milk the cow; I would bring help to you;
and if you were hard pressed, I would strike a blow for you.

O, ochone, and it's not with hunger
or with wanting food, or drink, or sleep,
that I am growing thin, and my life is shortened;
but it is the love of a young man has withered me away.

It is early in the morning that I saw him coming,
going along the road on the back of a horse;
he did not come to me; he made nothing of me;
and it is on my way home that I cried my fill.

When I go by myself to the Well of Loneliness,
I sit down and I go through my trouble;
when I see the world and do not see my boy,
he that has an amber shade in his hair.

It was on that Sunday I gave my love to you;
the Sunday that is last before Easter Sunday.
And myself on my knees reading the Passion;
and my two eyes giving love to you for ever.

O, aya! my mother, give myself to him;
and give him all that you have in the world;

get out yourself to ask for alms,
and do not come back and forward looking for me.

My mother said to me not to be talking with you today,
or tomorrow, or on the Sunday;
it was a bad time she took for telling me that;
it was shutting the door after the house was robbed.

My heart is as black as the blackness of the sloe,
or as the black coal that is on the smith's forge;
or as the sole of a shoe left in white halls;
it was you put that darkness over my life.

You have taken the east from me, you have taken the west from me;
you have taken what is before me and what is behind me;
you have taken the moon, you have taken the sun from me;
and my fear is great that you have taken God from me!

From The Kiltartan Poetry Book *(1918)*

This stunning translation of an 8th century Irish lament, in which a young woman pours out her sorrow at the man she loves going 'across the sea', is one of Lady Gregory's most enduring works.

'No Second Troy'
William Butler Yeats

Why should I blame her that she filled my days
With misery, or that she would of late
Have taught to ignorant men most violent ways,
Or hurled the little streets upon the great,
Had they but courage equal to desire?
What could have made her peaceful with a mind
That nobleness made simple as a fire,
With beauty like a tightened bow, a kind
That is not natural in an age like this,
Being high and solitary and most stern?
Why, what could she have done, being what she is?
Was there another Troy for her to burn?

From The Green Helmet and Other Poems *(1910)*

Yeats wrote this poem after his muse, Maud Gonne, married republican John MacBride. He evokes the mythological Trojan War, which began with a love triangle between King Menelaus of Sparta, his beautiful wife Helen, and Paris, prince of Troy.

'Maire My Girl'
John Keegan Casey

Over the dim blue hills
   Strays a wild river,
Over the dim blue hills
   Rests my heart ever.
Dearer and brighter than
   Jewels and pearl,
Dwells she in beauty there,
   Maire my girl.

Down upon Claris heath
   Shines the soft berry,
On the brown harvest tree
   Droops the red cherry.
Sweeter thy honey lips,
   Softer the curl
Straying adown thy cheeks,
   Maire my girl.

'Twas on an April eve
   That I first met her;
Many an eve shall pass
   Ere I forget her.
Since, my young heart has been
   Wrapped in a whirl,

Thinking and dreaming of
   Maire my girl.

She is too kind and fond
   Ever to grieve me,
She has too pure a heart
   E'er to deceive me.
Was I Tyrconnell's chief
   Or Desmond's earl,
Life would be dark, wanting
   Maire my girl.

Over the dim blue hills
   Strays a wild river,
Over the dim blue hills
   Rests my heart ever;
Dearer and brighter than
   Jewels or pearl,
Dwells she in beauty there,
   Maire my girl.

From A Wreath of Shamrocks *(1866)*

Known as the 'poet of the Fenians', John Keegan Casey was imprisoned for his part in the Rising of 1867. When he died, aged just twenty-four, up to a hundred thousand mourners walked in his funeral procession.

'The Stars Stand Up in the Air'
Anon, translated from the Irish by Thomas MacDonagh

The stars stand up in the air,
The sun and the moon are gone,
The strand of its waters is bare.
And her sway is swept from the swan.

The cuckoo was calling all day,
Hid in the branches above,
How my *stóirín* is fled far away –
'Tis my grief that I gave her my love!

Three things through love I see –
Sorrow and sin and death –
And my mind reminding me
That this doom I breathe with my breath.

But sweeter than violin or lute
Is my love – and she left me behind!
I wish that all music were mute,
And I to all beauty were blind.

She's more shapely than swan by the strand,
She's more radiant than grass after dew,
She's more fair than the stars where they stand –
'Tis my grief that her ever I knew!

From The Book of Irish Poetry, *ed. Alfred Perceval Graves (1914)*

Tipperary-born Thomas MacDonagh was a poet, educator and union leader who was executed for his part in the 1916 Rising.

'A Song'
Francis Ledwidge

My heart has flown on wings to you, away
In the lonely places where your footsteps lie
Full up of stars when the short showers of day
Have passed like ancient sorrows. I would fly
To your green solitude of woods to hear
You singing in the sounds of leaves and birds;
But I am sad below the depth of words
That nevermore we two shall draw anear.

Had I but wealth of land and bleating flocks
And barnfuls of the yellow harvest yield,
And a large house with climbing hollyhocks
And servant maidens singing in the field,
You'd love me; but I own no roaming herds,
My only wealth is songs of love for you,
And now that you are lost I may pursue
A sad life deep below the depth of words.

From Songs of the Fields *(1915)*

Francis Ledwidge wrote this poem after the woman he loved, who was from a prosperous farming family, broke off their friendship and married a wealthier man.

'Tutto è sciolto'
James Joyce

A birdless heaven, seadusk, one lone star
Piercing the west,
As thou, fond heart, love's time, so faint, so far,
Rememberest.

The clear young eyes' soft look, the candid brow,
The fragrant hair,
Falling as through the silence falleth now
Dusk of the air.

Why then, remembering those shy
Sweet lures, repine
When the dear love she yielded with a sigh
Was all but thine?

From Pomes Penyeach *(1927)*

The title of this poem can be translated as 'All is lost now' and is taken from the Bellini opera The Sleepwalker (La Sonnambula). *It is mentioned again in the 'Sirens' episode of* Ulysses, *where Leopold Bloom ponders this beautiful aria as he worries that his wife Molly is unfaithful.*

'In Tír-na-nÓg'
Ethna Carbery

> In Tír-na-nÓg,
> In Tír-na-nÓg,
>
> Summer and spring go hand in hand, and in the radiant weather
> Brown autumn leaves and winter snow come floating down together.

> In Tír-na-nÓg,
> In Tír-na-nÓg,
>
> The sagans sway this way and that, the twisted fern uncloses,
> The quicken-berry hides its red above the tender roses.

> In Tír-na-nÓg,
> In Tír-na-nÓg,
>
> The blackbird lilts, the robin chirps, the linnet wearies never,
> They pipe to dancing feet of *Sidhe* and thus shall pipe for ever.

> In Tír-na-nÓg,
> In Tír-na-nÓg,
>
> All in a drift of apple-blooms my true love there is roaming,
> He will not come although I pray from dawning until gloaming.

>   In Tír-na-nÓg,
>   In Tír-na-nÓg,

The *Sidhe* desired my Heart's Delight, they lured him from my keeping,
He stepped within a fairy ring while all the world was sleeping.

>   In Tír-na-nÓg,
>   In Tír-na-nÓg,

He hath forgotten hill and glen where misty shadows gather,
The bleating of the mountain sheep, the cabin of his father.

>   In Tír-na-nÓg,
>   In Tír-na-nÓg,

He wanders in a happy dream thro' scented golden hours,
He flutes, to woo a fairy love, knee deep in fairy flowers.

>   In Tír-na-nÓg,
>   In Tír-na-nÓg,

No memory hath he of my face, no sorrow for my sorrow,
My flax is spun, my wheel is hushed, and so I wait the morrow.

From The Four Winds of Eirinn *(1902)*
In Irish mythology, Tír-na-nÓg is the island paradise of eternal youth. It is best known from the story of Fianna warrior Oisín, who travels there after falling in love with Niamh Cinn-Óir.

'Destiny'
Speranza (Lady Jane Wilde)

I.
There was a star that lit my life —
  It hath set to rise no more,
For Heaven, in mercy, withdrew the light
  I fain would have knelt before.

II.
There was a flower I pluck'd in my dreams,
  Fragrant and fair to see;
Oh, would I had never awoke and found
  Such bloom not here for me.

III.
There was a harp, whose magic tone,
  Echoed my faintest words —
But Destiny's hand, with a ruthless touch,
  Hath rent the golden chords.

IV.
There was a path like Eden's vale,
  In which I was spell'd to stray,
But Destiny rose with a flaming sword
  To guard that path alway.

V.

I've looked on eyes were like the star —
  Their light is quench'd for me;
And a soul I have known like the golden harp
  That breath'd but melody.

VI.

And moments bright as that dream-land
  Where bloomed the radiant flower.
Oh! would I had died ere I felt the gloom
  Of this dark, joyless hour.

VII.

Fatal the time I rais'd mine eyes
  To eyes whose light hath blasted —
Yet ere I could turn from their glance away,
  Life had with gazing wasted.

VIII.

Bitter the thought that years may pass —
  Yet thus it must be ever,
To look on thy form, to hear thy voice —
  But nearer — never, never.

IX.

Could I but love as I love the stars,
  Or the gush of the twilight breeze,

Or the pale light of the wandering moon
   Glancing through forest trees;

X.

With a sinless, calm, untroubled love,
   Look upwards and adore —
Could I but thus gaze life away,
   Without the wish to soar.

XI.

In vain! in vain! I hope, I weep,
   I kneel the long nights in prayer —
Oh! better to die in the noon of life,
   Than love, and yet despair.

From Poems by Speranza *(1871)*

Lady Wilde was a political force in 19th century Dublin, writing rousing articles for The Nation *calling for armed conflict. She said of herself, 'I should like to rage through life — this orthodox creeping is too tame for me — ah, this wild rebellious ambitious nature of mine.'*

'To ———'

Thomas Moore

When I loved you, I can't but allow
I had many an exquisite minute;
But the scorn that I feel for you now
Hath even more luxury in it!

Thus, whether we're on or we're off,
Some witchery seems to await you;
To love you is pleasant enough,
And oh! 'tis delicious to hate you!

From Epistles, Odes, and Other Poems *(1806)*

When a reviewer of this collection called Thomas Moore 'the most licentious of modern versifiers', the poet challenged him to a duel. Police intervened and found there was no bullet in the reviewer's pistol — and there most likely wasn't one in Moore's either.

'The Song of Wandering Aengus'
William Butler Yeats

I went out to the hazel wood,
Because a fire was in my head,
And cut and peeled a hazel wand,
And hooked a berry to a thread;
And when white moths were on the wing,
And moth-like stars were flickering out,
I dropped the berry in a stream
And caught a little silver trout.

When I had laid it on the floor
I went to blow the fire aflame,
But something rustled on the floor,
And someone called me by my name:
It had become a glimmering girl
With apple blossom in her hair
Who called me by my name and ran
And faded through the brightening air.

Though I am old with wandering
Through hollow lands and hilly lands,
I will find out where she has gone,
And kiss her lips and take her hands;
And walk among long dappled grass,
And pluck till time and times are done
The silver apples of the moon,
The golden apples of the sun.

From The Wind Among the Reeds *(1899)*

The Irish god Aengus fell in love with a woman he had seen only in his dreams. Unlike Yeats's Aengus, who seems to search forever, the Aengus of myth eventually finds his love in real life, but she has been transformed into a swan.

'Do You Remember That Night?'
Anon, translated from the Irish by Eugene O'Curry

Do you remember that night
  That you were at the window,
  With neither hat nor gloves,
  Nor coat to shelter you;
  I reached out my hand to you,
  And you ardently grasped it,
  And I remained in converse with you
  Until the lark began to sing?

Do you remember that night
  That you and I were
  At the foot of the rowan tree,
  And the night drifting snow;
  Your head on my breast,
  And your pipe sweetly playing?
  I little thought that night
  Our ties of love would ever loosen.

O beloved of my inmost heart,
  Come some night, and soon,
  When my people are at rest,
  That we may talk together;
  My arms shall encircle you,
  While I relate my sad tale

> That it is your pleasant, soft converse
> That has deprived me of heaven.

> The fire is unraked,
>   The light extinguished,
>   The key under the door,
>   And do you softly draw it.
>   My mother is asleep,
>   And I am quite awake;
>   My fortune is in my hand,
>   And I am ready to go with you.

From Anthology of Irish Verse, *ed. Padraic Colum (1922)*

Born into a humble farming family in County Clare, Eugene O'Curry became a preeminent scholar of Irish and the co-author of the first dictionary of the Irish language.

'Inamorata'
Francis Ledwidge

The bees were holding levees in the flowers,
Do you remember how each puff of wind
Made every wing a hum? My hand in yours
Was listening to your heart, but now
The glory is all faded, and I find
No more the olden mystery of the hours
When you were lovely and our hearts would bow
Each to the will of each, but one bright day
Is stretching like an isthmus in a bay
From the glad years that I have left behind.

I look across the edge of things that were
And you are lovely in the April ways,
Holy and mute, the sigh of my despair ...
I hear once more the linnets' April tune
Beyond the rainbow's warp, as in the days
You brought me facefuls of your smiles to share
Some of your new-found wonders ... Oh when soon
I'm wandering the wide seas for other lands,
Sometimes remember me with folded hands,
And keep me happy in your pious prayer.

From Songs of the Fields *(1915)*

Ledwidge worked as a farmhand from an early age to support his widowed mother. He was inspired by the landscape of County Meath and would write down his poems wherever he could, even on fences, gates and stones.

'When You Are Old'
William Butler Yeats

When you are old and grey and full of sleep,
   And nodding by the fire, take down this book
   And slowly read, and dream of the soft look
Your eyes had once, and of their shadows deep.

How many loved your moments of glad grace,
   And loved your beauty with love false or true,
   But one man loved the pilgrim soul in you,
And loved the sorrows of your changing face.

And bending down beside the glowing bars
   Murmur, a little sad, 'From us fled Love.
   He paced upon the mountains far above,
And hid his face amid a crowd of stars.'

From The Countess Kathleen and Various Legends and Lyrics *(1892)*

W.B. Yeats wrote this in response to a 16th century poem by the French writer Pierre de Ronsard, 'Quand vous serez bien vieille', which also sees Ronsard's muse sitting by the fire thinking of the poet's erstwhile love for her.

'The Rose of Mooncoin'
Watt Murphy

How sweet 'tis to roam by the sunny Suir stream
And hear the dove's coo 'neath the morning's sunbeam,
Where the thrush and the robin their sweet notes entwine
On the banks of the Suir that flows down by Mooncoin.

Flow on, lovely river, flow gently along
By your waters so sweet sounds the lark's merry song.
On your green banks I'll wander where first I did join
With you, lovely Molly, the rose of Mooncoin.

Oh Molly, dear Molly, it breaks my fond heart
To know that we two forever must part.
I'll think of you, Molly, while sun and moon shine
On the banks of the Suir that flows down by Mooncoin.

Then here's to the Suir with its valley so fair
As oftimes we wandered in the cool morning air,
Where the roses are blooming and the lilies entwine
On the banks of the Suir that flows down by Mooncoin.

She has sailed far away o'er the deep rolling foam,
Far away from the hills of her dear Irish home,
Where the fisherman goes with his small boat and line
On the banks of the Suir that flows down by Mooncoin.

Flow on, lovely river, flow gently along
By your waters so sweet sounds the lark's merry song.
On your green banks I'll wander where first I did join
With you, lovely Molly, the rose of Mooncoin.

Written around 1850

Schoolteacher Watt Murphy, a Catholic, wrote this poem when the father of his beloved Molly, a Protestant, sent her to England to keep them apart. The two loved to walk together by the River Suir in Mooncoin, County Kilkenny.

'The Lowlands of Flanders'
Katharine Tynan

The night that I was married
  Our Captain came to me:
Rise up, rise up, new-married man
  And come at once with me.

For the Lowlands of Flanders,
  It's there that we must fight;
So look your last and buss your last,
  For we shall sail to-night.

'Tis all for our Counterie
  And for our King we go
To the Lowlands of Flanders
  Against the German foe.

The girl that weds a soldier
  Must never blench for fear;
I kissed my last and looked my last
  Upon my lovely dear.

The Lowlands of Flanders,
  Their rivers run so red.
But I must say Good-bye, my dear,
  My only dear, I said.

For now I must go sailing
  Upon the stormy main;
Good-bye, good-bye, my only Love,
  Till I shall come again.

I put her white arms from me,
  Her cheek was cold as clay.
The night that I was married
  No longer I might stay.

Our bugles they are blowing,
  And I must sail the sea,
For the Lowlands of Flanders
  Betwixt my love and me.

From Flower of Youth: Poems in War Time *(1915)*

With her two sons fighting in World War One, Katharine Tynan wrote many poignant verses about war and the people left behind. She also penned thousands of letters to the bereaved families of soldiers lost on the front lines.

"Tis the Last Rose of Summer'
Thomas Moore

'Tis the last rose of summer
Left blooming alone;
All her lovely companions
Are faded and gone;
No flower of her kindred,
No rosebud is nigh,
To reflect back her blushes,
Or give sigh for sigh.

I'll not leave thee, thou lone one,
To pine on the stem;
Since the lovely are sleeping,
Go sleep thou with them.
Thus kindly I scatter
Thy leaves o'er the bed,
Where thy mates of the garden
Lie scentless and dead.

So soon may *I* follow,
When friendships decay,
And from Love's shining circle
The gems drop away.
When true hearts lie wither'd,
And fond ones are flown,
Oh! who would inhabit
This bleak world alone?

From The Irish Melodies *(1808–1834)*

Thomas Moore wrote this poem in 1805 while staying in Jenkinstown Castle in County Kilkenny. He was apparently inspired by the late-blooming Rosa 'Old Blush', whose pale-pink petals turn darker at summer's end.

'And Then No More'
James Clarence Mangan

I saw her once, one little while, and then no more:
'Twas Eden's light on earth awhile, and then no more.
Amid the throng, she passed along the meadow-floor:
Spring seemed to smile on earth awhile, and then no more.
But whence she came, which way she went, what garb she
    wore,
I noted not; I gazed awhile, and then no more.

I saw her once, one little while, and then no more:
'Twas Paradise on earth awhile, and then no more:
Ah! what avail my vigils pale, my magic lore?
She shone before mine eyes awhile, and then no more.
The shallop of my peace is wrecked on Beauty's shore;
Near Hope's fair isle it rode awhile, and then no more!

I saw her once, one little while, and then no more:
Earth looked like Heaven a little while, and then no more.
Her presence thrilled and lightened to its inner core,
My desert breast, a little while, and then no more.
So may, perchance, a meteor glance at midnight o'er
Some ruined pile a little while, and then no more!

I saw her once, one little while, and then no more.
The earth was Peri-land awhile, and then no more.
O might I see but once again, as once before,

Through chance or wile, that shape awhile, and then no more!
Death soon would heal my griefs: this heart, now sad and sore,
Would beat anew a little while, and then no more!

From James Clarence Mangan: His Selected Poems *(1897)*

The 'Clarence' in this author's name was a nom de plume, and he employed many others during his writing life, including 'The man in the cloak'. Indeed, Mangan was known to wear a blue cloak, a witch's hat and huge green spectacles as he wandered around his native Dublin.

'The Little Yellow Road'
Joseph Campbell, taken down from Mícheál Mac Ruaidhrí

I am sick, sick,
No part of me sound;
The heart in my middle
Dies of its wound,
Pining the time
When she did stand
With me shoulder to shoulder
And hand in hand.

I travelled west
By the little yellow road
In the hope I might see
Where my Secret abode.
White were her two breasts,
Red her hair,
Guiding the cow
And the weaned calf, her care.

Until wind flows
From this stream west,
Until green plain spreads
On the withered crest,
And white fields grow
The heather above,
My heart will not find
Kindness from my love.

There's a flood in the river
Will not ebb till day,
And dread on me
That my love is away.
Can I live a month
With my heart's pain
Unless she will come
And see me again?

I drink a measure
And I drink to you,
I pay, I pay,
And I pay for two.
Copper for ale
And silver for beer –
And do you like coming
Or staying here?

From The Poem Book of the Gael, *ed. Eleanor Hull (1912)*

Despite not being able to read or write, Mícheál Mac Ruaidhrí from County Mayo amassed a vast knowledge of Irish folklore, music and song. He was friends with Éamon de Valera and worked as a gardener and teacher at Padraic Pearse's school.

'On Inisheer'
Ethna Carbery

    On Inisheer, on Inisheer,
    In the Spring-tide of the year,
You sought me, in your eyes love's rapture burning;
    And for the words you said,
    Above my drooping head,
My heart flew to you on the wings of yearning.

    On Inisheer, on Inisheer,
    I had never known a fear,
Nor a sorrow, nor a sigh to mar my laughter;
    Until that saddest day,
    When my true love sailed away,
And the sun grew dim, and darkness followed after.

    Why did you go, oh love,
    Ere the primrose peeped above
The scanty grass bleached with the wind salt-bitter?
    Here, by a cabin fire,
    Each with our heart's desire,
Had not the peace of home for us been fitter?

    Than you to pine afar
    Under the Southern Star,
And I to pine by Keevin's ruined altar,
    Watching the cliffs of Clare

       Fade in the evening air,
Telling my beads for you in tones that falter;

       Or by the holy well,
       Where as the darkness fell,
And out of dark the tender dawn came flowing
       In seas of silver light,
       You prayed the livelong night
That Christ would bless and guard you in your going.

       Some day He keeps in store
       You will return, *a-stor*,
Your curragh down our foaming current speeding
       From the welcome of your clan,
       On the rocks of Inishmaan,
To heal my wound of longing, ever bleeding.

       On Inisheer, on Inisheer,
       Love, I shall wait you here,
My radiant web of dreams through grey hours weaving,
       Until, the red gold won,
       And all your wandering done,
You take me to your heart and end my grieving.

From The Four Winds of Eirinn *(1902)*

Inisheer is the smallest and most easterly of the Aran Islands ('Inis Oirr' means 'east island'), located off the coast of County Clare.

'The Vision of Love'
AE (George William Russell)

The twilight fleeted away in pearl on the stream,
And night, like a diamond dome, stood still in our dream.
Your eyes like burnished stones or as stars were bright
With the sudden vision that made us one with the night.

We loved in infinite spaces, forgetting here
The breasts that were lit with life and the lips so near;
Till the wizard willows waved in the wind and drew
Me away from the fulness of love and down to you.

Our love was so vast that it filled the heavens up:
But the soft white form I held was an empty cup,
When the willows called me back to earth with their sigh,
And we moved as shades through the deep that was you and I.

From The Nuts of Knowledge: Lyrical Poems Old and New *(1903)*

Upon opening a book at a random page, George Russell says he felt the word 'Aeon' — meaning an energy from eternity — jump out at him. He adopted it as his pseudonym, but due to a typesetting error, it was shortened to (and henceforth kept as) AE.

'Her Voice'
Oscar Wilde

The wild bee reels from bough to bough
   With his furry coat and his gauzy wing.
Now in a lily-cup, and now
   Setting a jacinth bell a-swing,
      In his wandering;
Sit closer love: it was here I trow
      I made that vow,

Swore that two lives should be like one
   As long as the sea-gull loved the sea,
As long as the sunflower sought the sun —
   It shall be, I said, for eternity
      'Twixt you and me!
Dear friend, those times are over and done.
      Love's web is spun.

Look upward where the poplar trees
   Sway and sway in the summer air,
Here in the valley never a breeze
   Scatters the thistledown, but there
      Great winds blow fair
From the mighty murmuring mystical seas,
      And the wave-lashed leas.

Look upward where the white gull screams,
  What does it see that we do not see?
Is that a star? or the lamp that gleams
  On some outward voyaging argosy —
    Ah! can it be
We have lived our lives in a land of dreams!
    How sad it seems.

Sweet, there is nothing left to say
  But this, that love is never lost,
Keen winter stabs the breasts of May
  Whose crimson roses burst his frost,
    Ships tempest-tossed
Will find a harbor in some bay,
    And so we may.

And there is nothing left to do
  But to kiss once again, and part,
Nay, there is nothing we should rue,
  I have my beauty — you your Art,
    Nay, do not start,
One world was not enough for two
    Like me and you.

From Poems *(1881)*

This poem is a companion piece to the one on the next page, 'My Voice', which tells the story of the end of a love affair from the other side.

'My Voice'
Oscar Wilde

Within this restless, hurried, modern world
   We took our hearts' full pleasure – You and I,
And now the white sails of our ship are furled,
   And spent the lading of our argosy.

Wherefore my cheeks before their time are wan,
   For very weeping is my gladness fled,
Sorrow hath paled my lip's vermilion,
   And Ruin draws the curtains of my bed.

But all this crowded life has been to thee
   No more than lyre, or lute, or subtle spell
Of viols, or the music of the sea
   That sleeps, a mimic echo, in the shell.

From Poems *(1881)*

Oscar Wilde may have written these two poems in reaction to the breakup of his relationship with the beautiful Florence Balcombe, who would go on to marry his old friend Bram Stoker.

Index of first lines

A birdless heaven, seadusk, one lone star 77
A honey mist on a day of frost, in a dark oak wood, 64
A love all-commanding, all-withstanding 35
A shaft of fire that falls like dew, 18
As oftentimes the too resplendent sun 21
As the sweet blackberry's modest bloom, 52
Because we share our sorrows and our joys 49
Dear thoughts are in my mind 22
Do you remember that night 86
Going to Mass by the will of God, 32
Had I the heavens' embroidered cloths, 31
Here is the road that you must climb with me, 47
How sweet 'tis to roam by the sunny Suir stream 90
How sweet the answer Echo makes 64
I am sick, sick, 98
I saw her once, one little while, and then no more: 96
I went out to the hazel wood, 84
I would that we were, my beloved, white birds on the foam of the sea! 45
If I have you then I have everything 58
If thou'lt be mine, the treasures of air, 26
In the scented bud of the morning – O, 44
In Tír-na-nÓg, 78
Is it a month since I and you 43
It is far, and it is far, 17
Like a wave that roams the sea 11

My dove, my beautiful one,   16
My heart has flown on wings to you, away   76
My hope and my love,   42
Nothing but sweet music wakes   53
O cloud-pale eyelids, dream-dimmed eyes   10
O Dónal óg, if you go across the sea,   68
O my Dark Rosaleen,   60
O what to me the little room   59
O, it was out by Donnycarney   51
Oh, call it by some better name,   13
On Inisheer, on Inisheer,   100
Over the dim blue hills   72
Put your head, darling, darling, darling,   50
She casts a spell, oh, casts a spell!   14
Stella this day is thirty four,   48
The bees were holding levees in the flowers,   88
The day I knew you loved me we had lain   40
The jester walked in the garden: 19
The long day was bright,   56
The night that I was married   92
The red rose whispers of passion,   28
The stars stand up in the air,   74
The twilight fleeted away in pearl on the stream,   102
The water rushes – the water foams –   23
The white bloom of the blackthorn, she,   37
The wild bee reels from bough to bough   103
The world has many lovers, but the one   29
There was a star that lit my life –   80

This heart that flutters near my heart 41
This is the time when bit by bit 25
'Tis the last rose of summer 94
When I loved you, I can't but allow 83
When you are old and grey and full of sleep, 89
Where Lagan stream sings lullaby 54
Why should I blame her that she filled my days 71
Within this restless, hurried, modern world 105

Index of authors

Boyle O'Reilly, John 28
Brooke, Charlotte 52
Campbell, Joseph 54, 98
Carbery, Ethna 47, 78, 100
Ferguson, Sir Samuel 22, 50
Gore-Booth, Eva 11
Graves, Alfred Perceval 35
Gregory, Lady Augusta 32, 42, 68
Hull, Eleanor 37
Hyde, Douglas 14, 64
Joyce, James 16, 41, 51, 77
Keegan Casey, John 72
Ledwidge, Francis 53, 76, 88
MacDonagh, Thomas 74
Mangan, James Clarence 60, 96
Milligan, Alice 17
Moore, Thomas 13, 26, 64, 83, 94

Murphy, Watt 90
Ó Raifteirí, Antoine 32
O'Curry, Eugene 86
Plunkett, Joseph Mary 40, 49, 58
Russell, George William (AE) 18, 102
Sigerson, Dora 29
Stephens, James 44
Swift, Jonathan 48
Synge, John Millington 43
Tynan, Katharine 25, 92
Wilde, Lady Jane (Speranza) 23, 80
Wilde, Oscar 21, 103, 105
Wynne, Frances 56
Yeats, William Butler 10, 19, 31, 45, 59, 71, 84, 89

Also available from The O'Brien Press

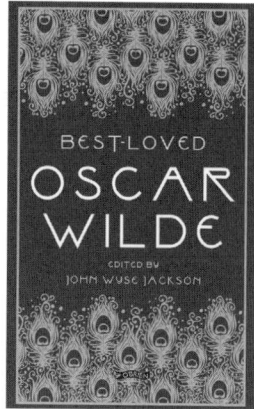
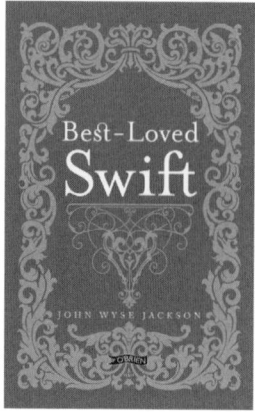

Great books from

Hundreds of books for all occasions

From beautiful gifts to books you'll want to keep forever! The best writing, wonderful illustration and leading design. Discover books for readers of all ages.

Follow us for all the latest news and information, or go to our website to explore our full range of titles.

 TheOBrienPress   TheOBrienPress

 OBrienPress   TheOBrienPress

Visit, explore, buy
obrien.ie

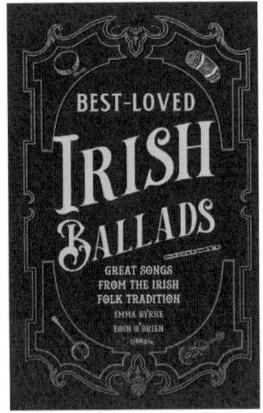

www.obrien.ie